T0419210

**LEADERS IN MY COMMUNITY**

# I WANT TO BE PRESIDENT

by Jennifer Boothroyd

Consultant: Beth Gambro
Reading Specialist, Yorkville, Illinois

Minneapolis, Minnesota

# Teaching Tips

## Before Reading

- Look at the cover of the book. Discuss the picture and the title.
- Ask readers to brainstorm a list of what they already know about the president. What can they expect to see in the book?
- Go on a picture walk, looking through the pictures to discuss vocabulary and make predictions about the text.

## During Reading

- Read for purpose. Encourage readers to think about leaders in their country as they are reading.
- Ask readers to look for the details of the book. What are they learning about the job of a president?
- If readers encounter an unknown word, ask them to look at the sounds in the word. Then, ask them to look at the rest of the page. Are there any clues to help them understand?

## After Reading

- Encourage readers to pick a buddy and reread the book together.
- Ask readers to name two things the president does. Find the pages that tell about these things.
- Ask readers to write or draw something they learned about being president.

**Credits:**
Cover and title page, © LightFieldStudios/iStock, © Orhan Cam/Shutterstock; 3, © Joseph Sohm/Shutterstock; 5, © Maksym Yemelyanov/Adobe Stock and © Antonio_Diaz/iStock; 6–7, © adamkaz/iStock; 8–9, © Jeff Kinsey/Shutterstock; 10–11, © Planetpix/Alamy; 12–13, © Ryan Rahman/Shutterstock; 14–15, © White House Photo / Alamy Stock Photo/Alamy; 17, © ZUMA Press, Inc. / Alamy Stock Photo/Alamy; 18–19, © Abaca Press / Alamy Stock Photo/Alamy; 21, © Monkey Business Images/Shutterstock; 22T, © OlgaKhorkova/Shutterstock; 22M, © wavebreakmedia/Shutterstock; 22B, © Bill Morson/Shutterstock; 22TL, © moodboard/Adobe Stock; 22TM, © dtiberio/Adobe Stock; 22TR, © Felipe Sanchez/Adobe Stock; 22BL, © betto rodrigues/Shutterstock; 22BR, © Krakenimages.com/Adobe Stock.

STATEMENT ON USAGE OF GENERATIVE ARTIFICIAL INTELLIGENCE
Bearport Publishing remains committed to publishing high-quality nonfiction books. Therefore, we restrict the use of generative AI to ensure accuracy of all text and visual components pertaining to a book's subject. See BearportPublishing.com for details.

*Library of Congress Cataloging-in-Publication Data*

Names: Boothroyd, Jennifer, 1972- author.
Title: I want to be president / by Jennifer Boothroyd.
Description: Bearcub books. | Minneapolis, Minnesota : Bearport Publishing
 Company, [2024] | Series: Leaders in my community | Includes
 bibliographical references and index.
Identifiers: LCCN 2023028925 (print) | LCCN 2023028926 (ebook) | ISBN
 9798889162667 (library binding) | ISBN 9798889162711 (paperback) | ISBN
 9798889162759 (ebook)
Subjects: LCSH: Presidents--United States--Juvenile literature. |
 Presidents--Juvenile literature.
Classification: LCC JK517 .B66 2024 (print) | LCC JK517 (ebook) | DDC
 352.230973--dc23/eng/20230711
LC record available at https://lccn.loc.gov/2023028925
LC ebook record available at https://lccn.loc.gov/2023028926

Copyright © 2024 Bearport Publishing Company. All rights reserved. No part of this publication may be reproduced in whole or in part, stored in any retrieval system, or transmitted in any form or by any means, electronic, mechanical, photocopying, recording, or otherwise, without written permission from the publisher.

For more information, write to Bearport Publishing, 5357 Penn Avenue South, Minneapolis, MN 55419.

# Contents

**I Want to Lead** .................... 4

Be a Leader Now ......................... 22

Glossary ................................. 23

Index .................................... 24

Read More ............................... 24

Learn More Online ....................... 24

About the Author ........................ 24

# I Want to Lead

Many people live in the United States.

The president leads everyone in our **country**.

I want to be president someday!

How could I get this big job?

The people of the United States **vote** for the president.

They pick who will be in charge.

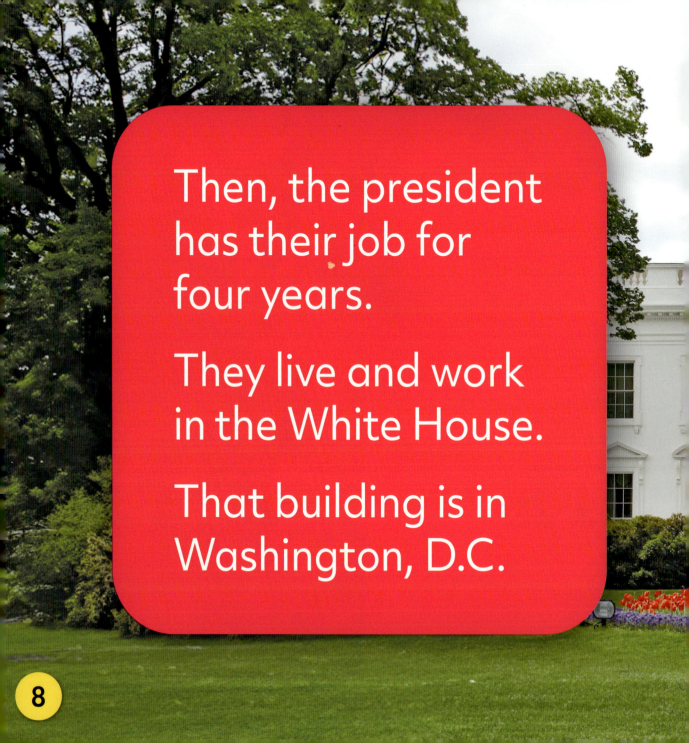

Then, the president has their job for four years.

They live and work in the White House.

That building is in Washington, D.C.

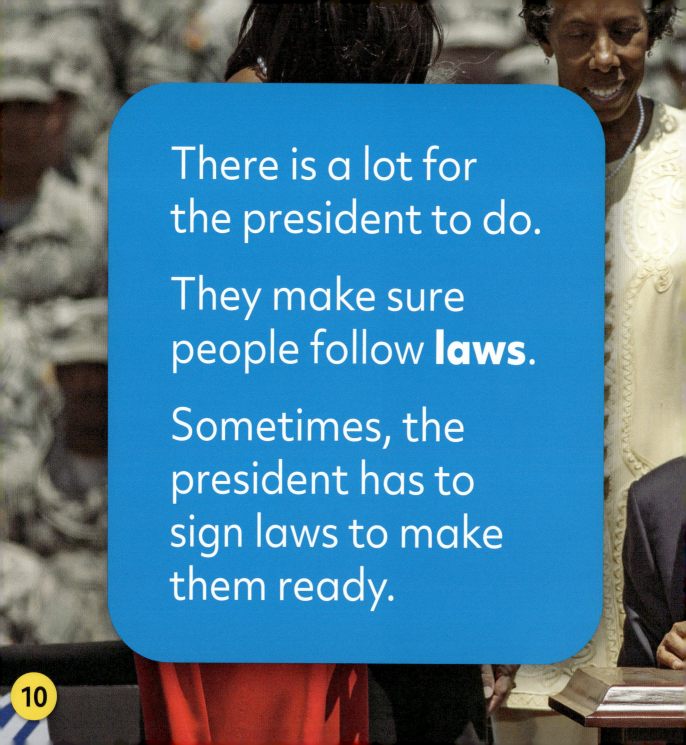

There is a lot for the president to do.

They make sure people follow **laws**.

Sometimes, the president has to sign laws to make them ready.

The president is in charge of the **military**, too.

These **soldiers** work to help keep our country safe.

Our president makes many **decisions**.

Often, they need help to make the best choices.

The president works with a team to get things done.

Say decisions like di-SIZH-uhnz

Everyone in our country is important to the president.

The president hears from people in every state.

They listen to what people want.

Sometimes, the president meets with leaders from other countries.

They work together to help the world.

Being the president is a lot of work.

Taking care of our country is a big job.

But I think I could do it!

# Be a Leader Now

There are many ways you can be a leader before you become president.

Write a letter or an email to the president. Share what you think is good for the country.

Learn about the United States. The more you know, the more you can do!

Write letters to people in the military. Thank them for their hard work.

# Glossary

**country** an area of land that has borders and rules for all the people there

**decisions** choices made about things

**laws** rules that people must follow

**military** the groups of soldiers that protect a country

**soldiers** people who fight or work for a country

**vote** to pick something as a group

## Index

**country** 4, 13, 16, 18, 20, 22
**laws** 10
**leaders** 18, 22
**military** 13, 22
**team** 14
**United States** 4, 6, 22
**vote** 6
**White House, the** 8–9

## Read More

**Bolinder, Mary Kate.** *Presidents (iCivics).* Huntington Beach, CA: Teacher Created Materials, 2022.

**Boothroyd, Jennifer.** *We Live in a Country (Where We Live).* Minneapolis: Bearport Publishing Company, 2024.

## Learn More Online

1. Go to **www.factsurfer.com** or scan the QR code below.
2. Enter **"To Be President"** into the search box.
3. Click on the cover of this book to see a list of websites.

## About the Author

Jenny Boothroyd has been to the White House, but she has never met a president. She has voted for president eight times.